D1707887

Think About It!

ACTIVITIES FOR TEACHING BASIC THINKING SKILLS

Middle Grades

By Imogene Forte

Thank You

to Mary Hamilton,
for drawing the pictures ...
to Dennas Davis,
for creating the cover ...
to Elaine Raphael,
for fixing it all up.

Library of Congress Catalog Card Number 80-84619
ISBN 0-913916-98-6

These Adventures In Thinking Belong To

_____

PREFACE

The time has
come, it
once was said,
To think of
many things ...
Of mysteries, mazes and puzzles;
Of curious ponderings;
And if your mind will let you soar
Like a butterfly on the wing.

If you've ever read <u>Alice In Wonderland</u>, those lines will probably sound familiar to you. They were borrowed from Lewis Carroll (and changed a little!) to show how much the world we live in is like Alice's Wonderland, and how we need to open our minds to it — to observe and test and think creatively, just as Alice did.

Today's busy world is filled with so many interesting places to go and fascinating things to do that we often rush through our "adventures in wonderland" without taking the time to think about them. It's only when we do stop to think that we realize how exciting each adventure really is. This book has been written to help you do just that — to stop and "Think About It." It's not a text book (though lots of study and research went into it); it's not a big, fat book that will take a long time to finish. It's just a collection of adventures through and about the wonderland we live in: pencil-and-paper activities, cut-and-paste projects, puzzles, games and fun pages to help you stretch your mind and look at things from a different point of view.

The first section of the book is called *PRELUDE* because "prelude" suggests "before" or "warming up to begin." The pages in this section have to do with your environment, with the people and the spaces around you. They will help you learn to function more effectively, and to become more aware of the wonderland of which you are a part. The middle section of the book is labeled *TESTING* because these pages will make you strain your mind and stretch your imagination. The puzzles and games here will test your logic and help you grow in "brain power." The name of the last section is *FLYING FREE*. These activities will help you enjoy your own creative powers as you think about ordinary things in extraordinary ways, and use new and different methods to do so.

As you go through this book, you'll often see the "Think About It" butterfly. When you find this symbol on a page, it means that it's time for YOU to get into action. It's your project from there on out. Read it, think about it, and "do your thing."

Now, follow the "Think About It" butterfly to your own adventures in wonderland. Take your time as you travel; look and listen, taste and touch with your mind. You'll soon find that you can do amazing things — if you'll just think about it.

Imogene Forte

HEY, THINKER!

When you have finished working through the pages in this book, you will have used all of the following reasoning skills:

Listening	Associating	Visualizing
Matching	Explaining	Combining
Recalling	Interviewing	Summarizing
Reading	Simulating	Creating
Collecting	Arranging	Designing
Observing	Interpreting	Encoding
Labeling	Scheduling	Refining
Identifying	Reporting	Inventing
Questioning	Categorizing	Substituting
Discovering	Inventorying	Composing
Describing	Calculating	Conceptualizing
Researching	Solving	Proposing
Locating	Relating	Organizing
Defining	Differentiating	Valuing
Responding	Comparing	Predicting
Sequencing	Contrasting	Discussing
Listing	Surveying	Selecting
Recording	Decoding	Projecting
Illustrating	Generalizing	Estimating
Sketching	Inferring	Rating
Diagramming	Extending	Criticizing
Brainstorming	Imagining	Deciding
Constructing	Hypothesizing	Defending
Experimenting	Formulating	Judging

Use the list as a skills check list. Decide as you go which page
(or pages) teaches which skill (or skills), and check them off as you work.

TABLE OF CONTENTS

PRELUDE

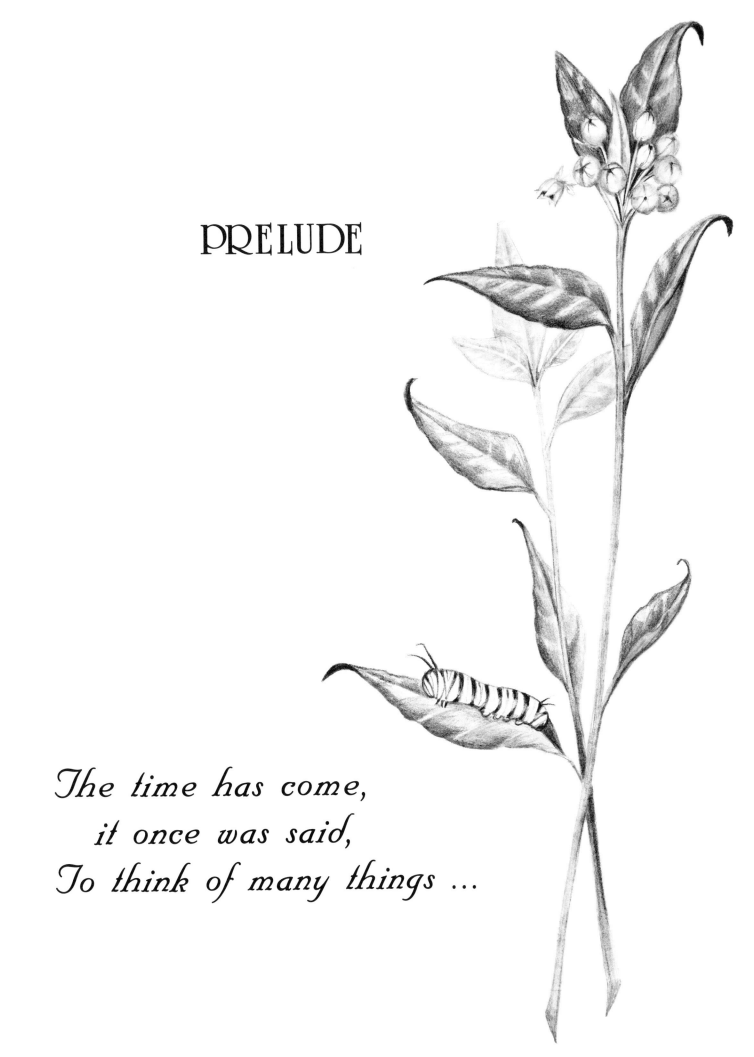

The time has come,
  it once was said,
To think of many things ...

A MARVELOUS MIGRATION

As summer draws to a close, the beautiful monarch butterflies start their journey south. It's not an easy journey. No one knows how they find their way over the mountains and deserts, or how they protect themselves from birds and other animals along the way. Any way you look at it, you have to see this journey as another one of the many marvels of nature.

Think About It Go to the library and find out as much as you can about the butterflies' journey. Share what you learn about this marvelous migration with somebody you like.

SYMBOLS SAY SOMETHING

Anthropologists tell us that people have always felt the need to communicate with other people, and to leave some sort of record of their existence.

Many years ago, people living in caves around the world drew pictures on the cave walls to tell of their lives and times. Instead of letters and numbers, they used symbols and signs.

 Think About It Draw a sign or symbol for each of these words.

LOVE: DEATH: TODAY:

SUNLIGHT: REVOLT: BIRTH:

OCEAN: PROGRESS: HATE:

FOREST: FIRE: HAPPINESS:

STORM: POLLUTION: DISEASE:

Use your symbols to write a message telling future generations about life in the 1980s.

_____

_____

_____

_____

_____

14

SUPER STUDENT

How do you rate as a student? Consider each question carefully before circling the rating that best describes you. Then add up your points and check your rating.

 I approach my studies by:

	Always	Sometimes	Almost Never
1. making a work schedule for each day.	2	1	0
2. checking to make sure my supplies are in order (pencils, paper, etc.).	2	1	0
3. keeping my desk or work area neat.	2	1	0
4. listening carefully when assignments are made.	2	1	0
5. asking good, well thought out questions.	2	1	0
6. participating in group discussions and brainstorming sessions.	2	1	0
7. trying to think of more than one solution to a problem and then selecting the best one.	2	1	0
8. checking my work for spelling, punctuation, and accuracy.	2	1	0
9. taking the time to recopy my work when necessary.	2	1	0
10. using my dictionary regularly.	2	1	0
11. asking for help only when I need it.	2	1	0
12. using good organizational skills (note taking, outlining, listening, etc.).	2	1	0
13. finishing my work on time.	2	1	0
14. making good use of the library.	2	1	0
Total	____ +	____ =	____

Check YOUR rating:
28—Super Student
22 to 27—Good Student
19 to 21—Fair Student
Below 19—Improvement Needed

THE SPOKEN WORD

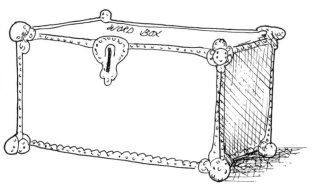

Choose a noun (the name of a person, place or thing) that has a sound you like. Write your word on the word box, but do not tell it to anyone.

Estimate the number of times you think you can cause the people around you to use your chosen word during the day. Write your estimate on the estimate box.

In this record box, write the name of each person who uses your word and the time of day it was used. At the end of the day, count the names in the box, and compare that number with your estimate.

Name:

Time of Day:

Special Delivery!

From Me To Myself

Write yourself a letter of encouragement.

Think About It — Begin by stating the problem that bothers you most right now. Tell what you think caused the problem and how it developed. Then, tell what you think you can do about it, and express confidence in your ability to solve the problem. Try to make this letter honest, but say what you want to hear, too.

When you finish your letter, reread it to see if your problem sounds as big as you thought. Fold up your letter, put it in your notebook and don't look at it again for a week.

At the end of the week, take it out, read it and decide if the letter helped you solve your problem.

Product Pizzazz

Mr. Phil N. Order is making up his new mail-order catalog. He hopes that this catalog will bring in more orders than the last one.

He knows that his catalog illustrations and descriptions are dull, but he isn't sure what to do about it.

Here is one page from his catalog. Can you help?

Think About It — Study the catalog page, and try to develop more exciting descriptions and containers for the items shown.

Remember, Mr. Phil N. Order's object is to sell the product.

Read Before You Buy

Smart shoppers are label readers.

Read the paragraphs below, and complete the labels. Include all important information.

The sweater Mary wants to buy was hand-knit by a very old lady. The lady makes all her sweaters out of a pre-shrunk, all-wool yarn. She uses only one pattern which is a size 12, cardigan style. She reminds everyone to wash these sweaters by hand only.

These oranges were grown in central Florida. They were ripened on the tree and were hand picked, packaged, and sold by the Ripe & Juicy Co. The bag contains 12 oranges.

QUESTION TIME

You are to be the chairman of a student group to present a panel discussion on discipline for a school assembly. This is a very important assignment since the principal and all teachers in the school will be present.

One student from each class will be nominated as a panel participant. Since you are chairman, it is your job to interview the nominees and select the three best qualified participants.

 Make a list of 7 to 10 good questions you will use to interview the participants.

Don't PANIC ~ PLAN It!

Select and circle one of the following subjects about which you would like to learn more.

jungle animals
space exploration
world geography

history of television
desert plant life
ocean farming

Number the following activities in the order in which they would be most helpful to you if you had only three days in which to prepare a class report.

_____ reading library books

_____ working with a group of your classmates

_____ reading magazine and newspaper articles

_____ studying a text book

_____ watching T.V. programs

_____ studying with one other person

_____ listening to the radio

_____ using encyclopedias and other reference books

Now, write a 5-step plan for learning as much about your chosen subject as possible in three days.

1. _____
_____

2. _____
_____

3. _____
_____

4. _____
_____

5. _____
_____

VOCABULARY VITAMINS

Do you tend to use the same old words over and over in your speaking and writing? Are you a tiny bit lazy about seeking out and using new words? Or do you just not think about it?

Maybe your vocabulary needs vitamins.

Get started on a vocabulary-health improvement plan to zip up your tired vocabulary. Fill the vitamin bottle below with colorful and exciting words that you don't ordinarily use. After your bottle is full, take a "dose" by using each word in either speaking or writing within the next three days.

Good, Good, Good!

Teachers are always giving awards to kids. They give awards for good work, good sportsmanship, good discipline, good health habits and other good things kids do.

SOMETIMES THEY GIVE BLUE RIBBONS

... OR GOOD SMELLING STICKERS

... OR SMILING FACES ON YOUR VERY GOOD PAPERS.

Whatever it is, the kid who gets the award feels fine, because he or she knows that the teacher has seen and appreciated his or her good work.

Wonder why kids never think of giving awards to teachers?

Think of one really neat thing that your teacher does that no other teacher you know does. Describe this very special thing.

_____

_____

_____

Now, design an award for your teacher. Show your work here.

P.S. GIVE THIS PAPER TO YOUR TEACHER.

2 POINTS of VIEW

IT'S AMAZING HOW DIFFERENTLY
TWO PEOPLE CAN FEEL ABOUT
THE SAME SET OF CIRCUMSTANCES.

Think About It Write the full name of the one person in your class who is closest to your own age.

_____

Your Birth Date _____ Time of Birth _____

Other Person's Birth Date _____ Time of Birth _____

    In three sentences, describe a controversial current event of interest to you and your classmates.

_____

_____

_____

_____

_____

    Interview the person nearest your own age to get his/her point of view on the issue.

My Point of View	His/Her Point of View
_____	_____
_____	_____
_____	_____
_____	_____

Compare and contrast the two points of view.

_____

_____

_____

_____

TELL-TALE BAGS

Sometimes you can tell a lot about a person by the things she or he carries around. What do these bags tell you about their owners?

Study each bag and its contents carefully. Draw a portrait in each frame to show how you think the owner looks. Write a description of each owner (age, sex, personality, height, weight, etc.,) on the lines given in each picture.

OBJECT: OBSERVATION

What color are your teacher's eyes?

_____

How many pictures are on the wall of your classroom?

_____

What size are the shoes you are wearing?

_____

What day of the week was your last birthday on?

_____

Write the names of three left-handed people you know.

_____

_____

_____

How tall is your best friend?

_____

How many colors are on the cover of your math book?

_____

How many trees are in your front yard?

_____

Words of Admiration

WRITE THE FULL NAME OF ONE PERSON IN YOUR CLASS THAT YOU ADMIRE A GREAT DEAL.

NAME: _____

Think About It

Write the three things about this person that you admire the most.

_____

_____

_____

Now, write a brief character sketch of the person. Be sure to include colorful information and descriptive phrases to convey to other people the admiration that you feel.

Hospital Line-Up

11 employees of Get Better Fast Hospital lined up to have this picture taken. Their proud smiles reflect the pride each person takes in a job well done.

Had you realized before how many working people it takes to make a hospital run smoothly?

Think About It

List the job of each person in this photograph.

1. _____   6. _____

2. _____   7. _____

3. _____   8. _____

4. _____   9. _____

5. _____   10. _____

11. _____

Circle one of the jobs you listed. On a sheet of paper, write a paragraph telling what you think the consequences would be if this job were not done for one week.

SPRUCE UP Your Sentences

Good self-expression is one mark of an interesting person. Write down the name of one person whose sentences are colorful enough to hold your attention most of the time.

_____

Think About It

"Spruce up" some sentences of your own. In each line below, there are four letters. Use each as the first letter of an interesting or colorful word, and make a complete sentence of them. Do not use any word more than once.

(If you want a real challenge, select one of the three subjects listed, and write all your sentences about that subject.)

— stormy weather
— space exploration
— famous sports figures

1. F _____	A _____	B _____	S _____
2. S _____	A _____	B _____	F _____
3. B _____	A _____	S _____	F _____
4. A _____	B _____	S _____	F _____
5. B _____	F _____	A _____	S _____
6. F _____	B _____	S _____	A _____
7. S _____	F _____	A _____	B _____
8. A _____	S _____	F _____	B _____

The Good Life Ahead

PARENT
GOOD CITIZEN
MISSIONARY
PUBLIC SERVANT
POLITICIAN
MILLIONAIRE
WELL-EDUCATED
PRIVATE EYE

GARDENER
FRIEND TO MANY
WORLD TRAVELLER
GLAMOROUS
MUSICIAN
CITY DWELLER
CRAFTSMAN
ATHLETE

Even though we don't know exactly what the future holds, it's never too early to begin looking ahead and planning for what we hope to achieve in later life.

 Think About It

From the fortune-teller's list, select five things that you think you might like to be when you grow up. Write them in the crystal ball below, and add five more of your own.

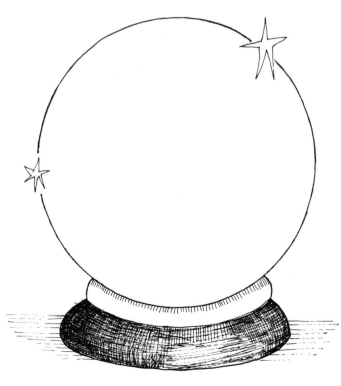

Now, gaze into your crystal ball, and think about the kind of life you have "planned" for yourself by your choices. List three things you could do now to begin preparing for this future.

1. _____

_____

2. _____

_____

3. _____

_____

GLAD TO BE ME

There are some very special things about every person in the world. Some are tall, some are short, some are thin, some are fat ... oh, you know, the list could go on and on.

The funny part is ...

some thin people wish they were fatter.
some fat people wish they were thinner.
some tall people wish they were shorter.
some short people wish they were taller.

Everybody seems to want to be different from what he or she is in some way.

But maybe,
just maybe,
there are some people in the world who like the way
they are just fine.

How about you?

Fill the "Glad to be Me" box with some of the things about you that make you glad to be you. Maybe you'll want to list people you know, things you do, talents you have, games you play, places you go (like school), feelings you have, things you own and more.

Use words (and pictures, if you like) to show the things that make you a very special person.

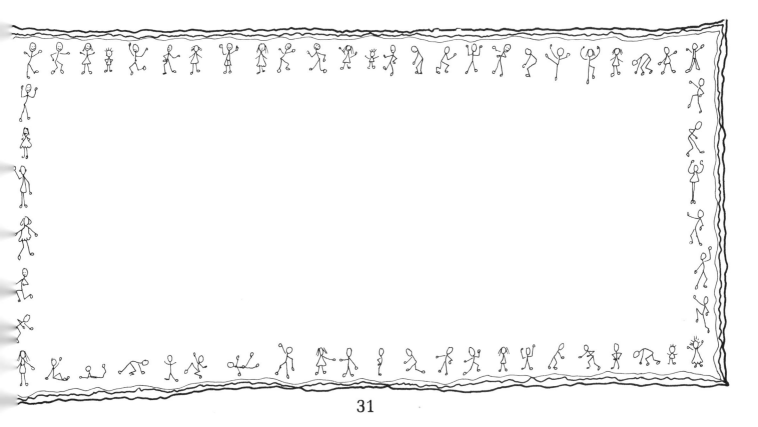

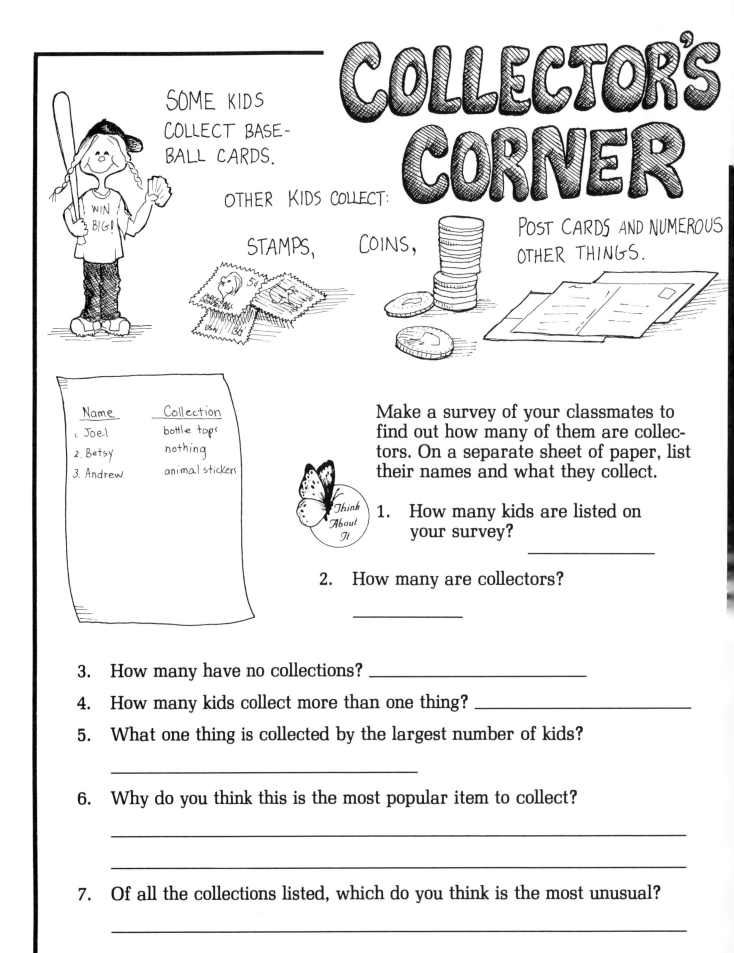

COLLECTOR'S CORNER

SOME KIDS COLLECT BASEBALL CARDS.

OTHER KIDS COLLECT:

STAMPS,   COINS,   POST CARDS AND NUMEROUS OTHER THINGS.

Name	Collection
1. Joel	bottle tops
2. Betsy	nothing
3. Andrew	animal stickers

Make a survey of your classmates to find out how many of them are collectors. On a separate sheet of paper, list their names and what they collect.

Think About It

1. How many kids are listed on your survey? _____

2. How many are collectors? _____

3. How many have no collections? _____

4. How many kids collect more than one thing? _____

5. What one thing is collected by the largest number of kids?

_____

6. Why do you think this is the most popular item to collect?

_____

_____

7. Of all the collections listed, which do you think is the most unusual?

_____

CRITICS' CHOICE

The books on the Critics' Choice Book Shelf are ones smart kids can't afford to miss. Plan for time to read or review each one. (You have probably read a lot of them already, so simply thumb through those and reread the special parts.)

As you finish each book, select the rating code that you feel best describes it, and write it in the space under the book. When you have finished, you will qualify as a Critic of Renown.

RATING CODE:

RA- Read Again   OK- O.K.   M- Marvelous   D- Disappointing

TESTING

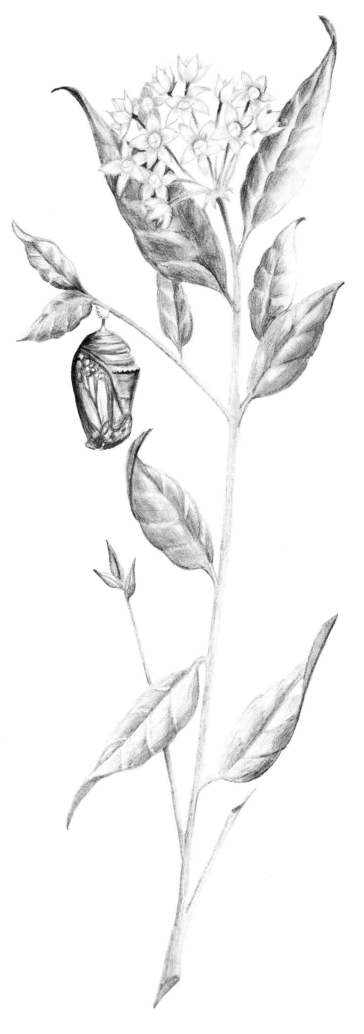

*Of mysteries, mazes
and puzzles;
Of curious
ponderings;*

The Missing Monarch

Find the beautiful monarch butterfly that is trapped in this picture by coloring all spaces containing the letters in the word "butterfly." Color the spaces containing consonants orange and the spaces containing vowels black.

THREE-MINUTE TASKS

What can you do in three minutes?

Give yourself three minutes flat to complete the following tasks.

1. Write the names of 11 things beginning with the letters x, y or z.

2. In Roman Numeral form, write only the odd numbers from 3 to 33.

3. Draw a picture of a zebra with 17 white stripes and 13 black stripes.

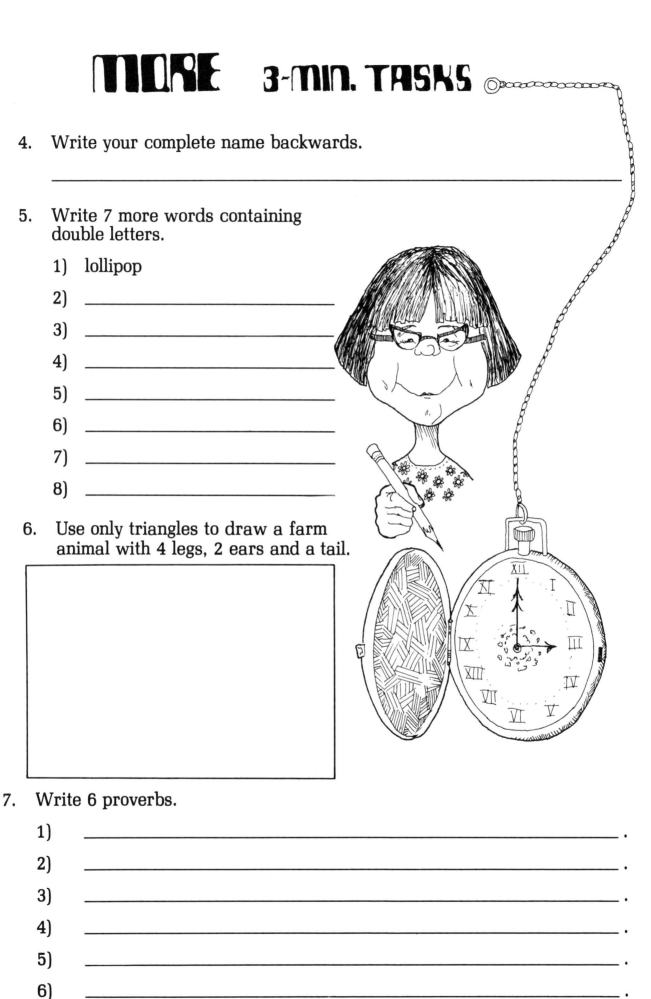

4.   Write your complete name backwards.

_____

5.   Write 7 more words containing
     double letters.

   1) lollipop

   2) _____

   3) _____

   4) _____

   5) _____

   6) _____

   7) _____

   8) _____

6.   Use only triangles to draw a farm
     animal with 4 legs, 2 ears and a tail.

7.   Write 6 proverbs.

   1) _____ .

   2) _____ .

   3) _____ .

   4) _____ .

   5) _____ .

   6) _____ .

Are You Sure?

READ EACH OF THE ELEVEN SENTENCES BELOW ONE TIME ONLY. QUICKLY DECIDE IF YOU THINK EACH STATEMENT IS TRUE OR FALSE, AND MARK THE APPROPRIATE COLUMN.

	T	F
1. A beaver can fell a tree 5" in diameter in 3 minutes.		
2. Zebras come from northern Africa.		
3. A ukulele is a small guitar with 5 strings.		
4. Uranus is the third largest planet.		
5. The saber-toothed tiger still lives in some parts of the world.		
6. A vassal received land and protection from a Lord during the Middle Ages.		
7. Bats are the only mammals that fly.		
8. A stalactite is formed by the dripping of water containing chlorine.		
9. Unicorns live in the jungles of Africa.		
10. Spacecraft have landed on Mars, Venus, Mercury, Saturn and Jupiter.		
11. Light has a velocity of about 186,000 miles per second.		

Think About It

Go back and reread each statement. Question your True/False decisions. Circle any that you are undecided about on your second reading.

Turn this page upside down and check the answers to find out how well you did.

BONUS!!
Now you can add these facts to your memory bank!

T — 1, 4, 6, 7, 11.   F — 2, 3, 5, 8, 9, 10.

40

MEMORY BANK

Memorizing information that is apt to be used often is like putting money in the bank. It's always there when you need it, and all you have to do is draw it out.

A little practice in memorizing poetry is a good way to begin adding to your Memory Bank Account.

1. Write the name of the longest poem you can recite from memory.

_____

2. Select a poem from a textbook or library book that you think you can memorize in 10 minutes. Write the name of the poem and its author here.

_____

3. Time yourself while you study the poem. Close your book and try to repeat the poem from memory. How well did you do?

____Memorized whole poem ____Almost made it ____Need to try again

4. Thumb through your books, and find three more poems you'd like to add to your account. Write their names and the names of their authors here.

1) _____

2) _____

3) _____

SOME GOOD ADVICE

WHEN DANNY DOBETTER WENT AWAY TO CAMP, HIS FATHER USED THIS CODE TO WRITE POST CARDS TO HIM.

A - N	H - T	O - K	W - J
B - U	I - X	P - B	X - G
C - 5	J - Z	Q - F	Y - D
D - V	K - R	R - C	Z - A
E - Q	L - O	S - H	
F - W	M - Y	T - I	
G - P	N - L	U - M	V - E

Danny Dobetter
Mosquito Lake Camp
Mosquito Lake, MT 27500

Think About It

DECODE THE MESSAGES.

VZKNM HL PVY, VZKNM HL KTCV UZOVC
Z UZA SVZNHSM , FVZNHSM ZAY FTCV.

_____
_____
_____
_____
_____
_____

Z GVAAM CZDVY TC Z GVAAM VZKAVY.
Z QLLN ZAY STC ULAVM ZKV CLLA
GZKHVY.

_____
_____
_____
_____
_____
_____
_____

NVH MLBK RLACRTVARV PV MLBK XBTYV.
ALPLYM NLDVC Z NTHHVK PBX. SZCHV
UZOVC FZCHV.

_____
_____
_____
_____
_____

NLLO PVQLKV MLB NVZG. ZNN HSZH
XNTHHVKC TC ALH XLNY. HSTAXC ZKV
ALH ZC HSVM CVVU.

_____
_____
_____
_____
_____

Dear Dad,

DANNY DOBETTER IS A LAZY BUT LOYAL SON. HE ANSWERED EACH OF HIS FATHER'S POST CARDS USING THIS CODE.

A-F	H-L	O-Y	U-P
B-G	I-V	P-H	V-S
C-M	J-O	Q-C	W-X
D-Z	K-T	R-E	X-U
E-I	L-Q	S-K	Y-R
F-A	M-B	T-J	Z-W
G-N	N-D		

Think About It

ON A SEPARATE PIECE OF PAPER, WORK OUT RESPONSES TO MR. DOBETTER'S LETTERS. COPY YOUR CODED MESSAGES ON THE CARDS BELOW, & WRITE THE DECODED MESSAGES UNDER EACH ONE.

Scramble Ramble!

All 22 words listed below name wheeled items. The letters have been scrambled to challenge you to some quick thinking.

Time yourself to see how long it takes you to meet this "Scramble Ramble" challenge by unscrambling each word and writing its correct spelling in the appropriate blank space.

lomaiboute — _____

mootcoveil — _____

rottcar — _____

comtlecyro — _____

doeartbask — _____

usb — _____

anv — _____

yiblcec — _____

kofr flit — _____

besocoa — _____

elictcry — _____

kurct — _____

larrite — _____

yelcunci — _____

garerica — _____

rerewowbahl — _____

tarc — _____

ostecor — _____

lyldo — _____

takes — _____

gygub — _____

ownga — _____

You Do The Scrambling

Thinking of 22 words in one category is not as easy as it sounds. Select one of the following categories to use as a heading for your scrambled word list.

—vegetables   —trees
—countries   —spices
—minerals   —fish
        —insects

Give yourself 10 minutes to write a list of 22 scrambled words in your chosen category for a friend to unscramble.

1) _____ - _____

2) _____ - _____

3) _____ - _____

4) _____ - _____

5) _____ - _____

6) _____ - _____

7) _____ - _____

8) _____ - _____

9) _____ - _____

10) _____ - _____

11) _____ - _____

12) _____ - _____

13) _____ - _____

14) _____ - _____

15) _____ - _____

16) _____ - _____

17) _____ - _____

18) _____ - _____

19) _____ - _____

20) _____ - _____

21) _____ - _____

22) _____ - _____

Antonyms in Abundance

Read over the word list at the bottom of the scroll. Find and circle those words in the puzzle by looking across, down and diagonally. There are no backward words.

Make your own puzzle by using an antonym (opposite) for each of the words you have just circled. Write your words at the bottom of the scroll before you begin.

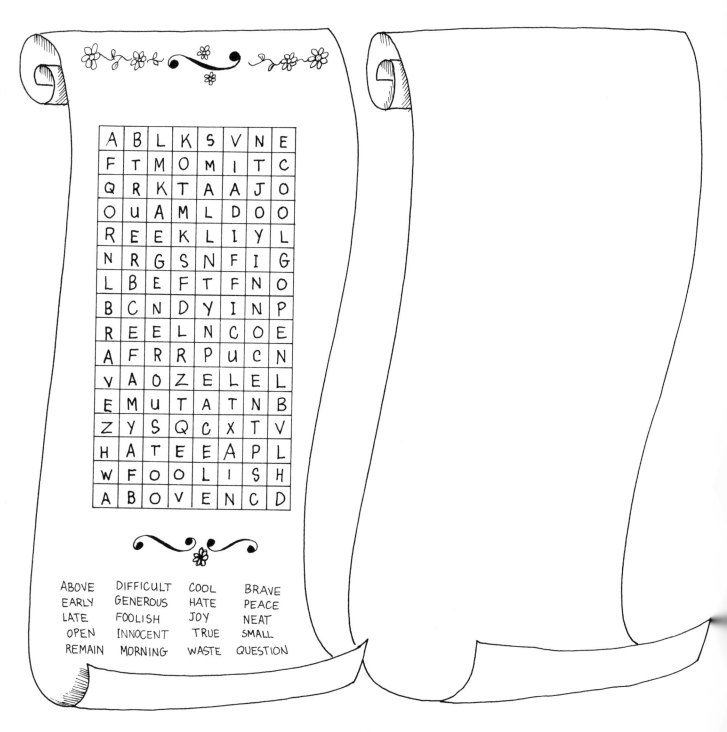

A	B	L	K	S	V	N	E
F	T	M	O	M	I	T	C
Q	R	K	T	A	A	J	O
O	U	A	M	L	D	O	O
R	E	E	K	L	I	Y	L
N	R	G	S	N	F	I	G
L	B	E	F	T	F	N	O
B	C	N	D	Y	I	N	P
R	E	E	L	N	C	O	E
A	F	R	R	P	U	C	N
V	A	O	Z	E	L	E	L
E	M	U	T	A	T	N	B
Z	Y	S	Q	C	X	T	V
H	A	T	E	E	A	P	L
W	F	O	O	L	I	S	H
A	B	O	V	E	N	C	D

ABOVE	DIFFICULT	COOL	BRAVE
EARLY	GENEROUS	HATE	PEACE
LATE	FOOLISH	JOY	NEAT
OPEN	INNOCENT	TRUE	SMALL
REMAIN	MORNING	WASTE	QUESTION

Phillip's Folly

Phillip the Painter painted these two pictures as presents for his twin sisters, Phyllis and Phyllene. Since the sisters are identical twins, Phillip wanted the pictures to be identical, too.

He painted the first picture for Phyllis and tried to copy it exactly for Phyllene. Alas, poor Phillip simply could not produce two identical pictures.

Phillip's aunt Phillistine made both sisters (and their brother) very unhappy by pointing out 21 differences in the pictures.

Think About It

Find and circle the 21 differences in Phyllene's picture.

Phyllis

Phyllene

47

ABSENT~MINDED PROFESSOR

Professor I. Furgot is the best chemist in town, but he does sometimes tend to forget what he's doing and take a snooze. As you can see, this time he fell asleep right in the middle of an experiment.

Find and circle 10 potential trouble spots that could cause big problems before the professor awakes.

A Double Value Puzzle

Here's a double value puzzle for you. First, the puzzle will be fun to solve. It will also give you a good math review.

Cut out all puzzle pieces. Put them together and paste on a sheet of paper. Then, solve the math problems.

Think About It

12x ___ = 8

9x ___ = 6

8x ___ = 8

7x ___ = 1

8x ___ = 8

8x ___

7x

7x

7x

8x ___ = 6

7x ___ = 1

12x ___ = 8

6x ___ = 9

8 = ___

2 = ___

9x

6 = ___

6 = ___

5x

6x

9x

5x

5 = ___

5 = ___

8 = ___

9x

7 = ___

12x

6 = ___

A Double Value Puzzle

YOU SHOULD KNOW

Read each statement. Decide whether it is true or false, and put a check in the correct box beside it.

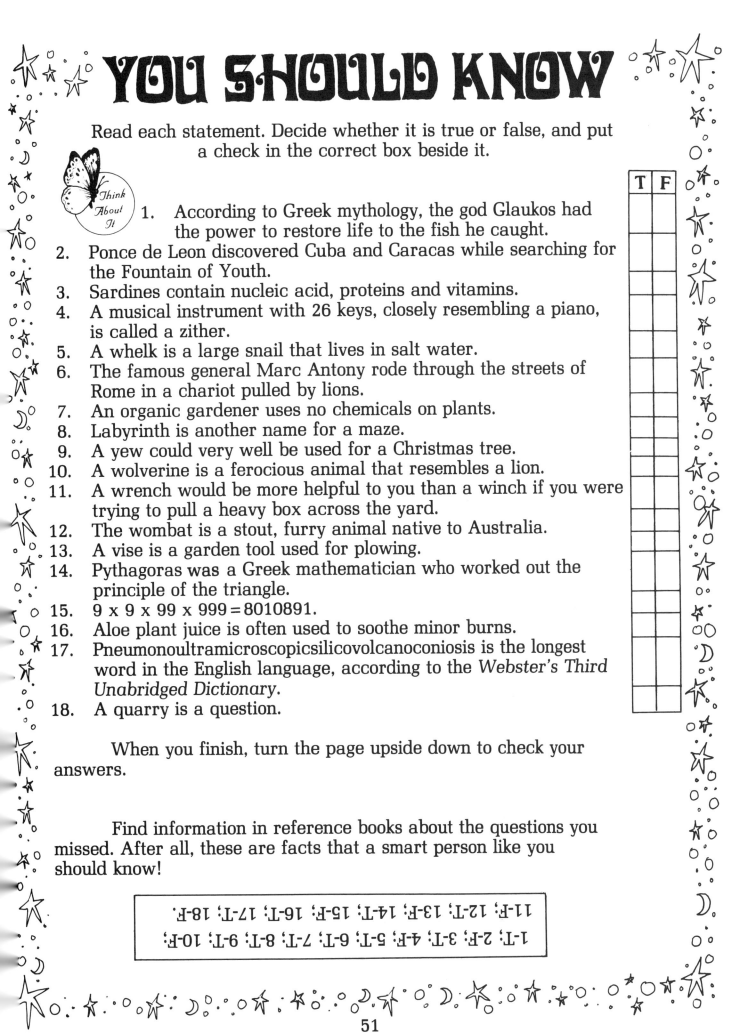

Think About It

	T	F
1.		
2.		
3.		
4.		
5.		
6.		
7.		
8.		
9.		
10.		
11.		
12.		
13.		
14.		
15.		
16.		
17.		
18.		

1. According to Greek mythology, the god Glaukos had the power to restore life to the fish he caught.
2. Ponce de Leon discovered Cuba and Caracas while searching for the Fountain of Youth.
3. Sardines contain nucleic acid, proteins and vitamins.
4. A musical instrument with 26 keys, closely resembling a piano, is called a zither.
5. A whelk is a large snail that lives in salt water.
6. The famous general Marc Antony rode through the streets of Rome in a chariot pulled by lions.
7. An organic gardener uses no chemicals on plants.
8. Labyrinth is another name for a maze.
9. A yew could very well be used for a Christmas tree.
10. A wolverine is a ferocious animal that resembles a lion.
11. A wrench would be more helpful to you than a winch if you were trying to pull a heavy box across the yard.
12. The wombat is a stout, furry animal native to Australia.
13. A vise is a garden tool used for plowing.
14. Pythagoras was a Greek mathematician who worked out the principle of the triangle.
15. 9 x 9 x 99 x 999 = 8010891.
16. Aloe plant juice is often used to soothe minor burns.
17. Pneumonoultramicroscopicsilicovolcanoconiosis is the longest word in the English language, according to the *Webster's Third Unabridged Dictionary*.
18. A quarry is a question.

When you finish, turn the page upside down to check your answers.

Find information in reference books about the questions you missed. After all, these are facts that a smart person like you should know!

1-T; 2-F; 3-T; 4-F; 5-T; 6-T; 7-T; 8-T; 9-T; 10-F; 11-F; 12-T; 13-F; 14-T; 15-F; 16-T; 17-T; 18-F.

Test your "word ability" with these word pyramids.

Start at the top and work to the word on the bottom line.
Add only one new letter to each row to make a new word.
Rearrange the letters any time you wish.

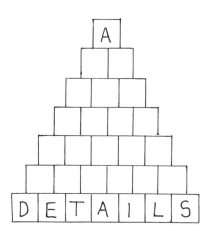

A

D E T A I L S

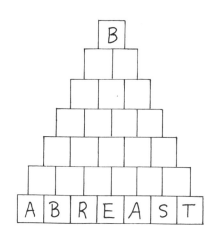

B

A B R E A S T

I

E N L I S T S

Now, pull some "Pyramid Pranks" of your own. Choose any letter you wish to put in each top space, and work your way down. Make sure each line is a complete word.

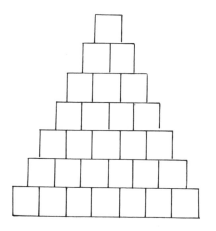

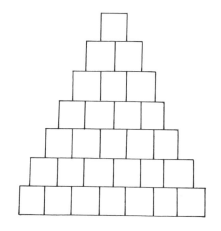

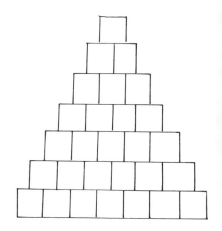

Yarn Alarm

Poor Mrs. Anders! While she was working away on her knitting, her cat tangled up her last ball of yarn. Now she must stop and untangle the mess before she can finish her project.

Can you help by finding and marking the way from the string's end back to the ball of yarn? Give it a try!

Think About It

(HINT: YOU MAY FOLLOW THE PATHS THAT GO OVER AND UNDER, BUT BEWARE OF THE ONES THAT STOP ALTOGETHER!)

A Figurative Memory

- Look at these figures for just 3 minutes.

- Cover this page with a clean sheet of paper, and try to draw the figures exactly as you remember them.

- Check your work to see how well you did.

- Try the test again if you feel you need more practice.

OH, CANADA!

Fill in the puzzle with the names of the capitals of the provinces of Canada listed below.

ACROSS:

2. Prince Edward Island
4. Northwest Territories
5. Nova Scotia
6. Newfoundland
8. Quebec
10. New Brunswick
11. Ontario
12. Saskatchewan

DOWN:

1. Yukon Territory
3. Manitoba
7. British Columbia
9. Alberta

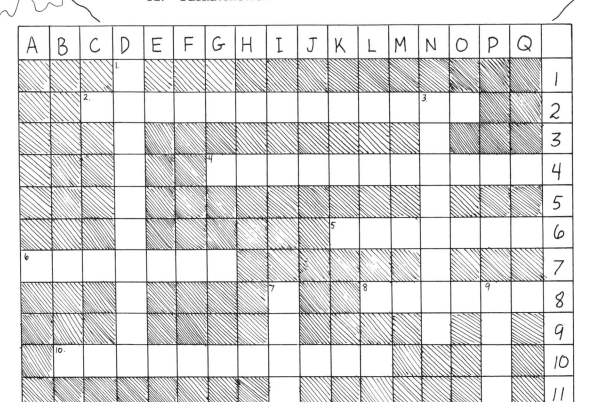

Use the letters at the grid points listed below to spell out the national capital of Canada.

1) H-2   2) D-4   3) P-13   4) L-6   5) N-2   6) I-15

___ ___ ___ ___ ___ ___
 1   2   3   4   5   6

Rivers of Renown!

All of the clues to this puzzle describe famous rivers.

Read the clues and fill in the names of the rivers. (Hint: Each of the names in the border has a place in the puzzle.)

Think About It

DANUBE, ELBE, FRASER, IRRAWADDY, MISSISSIPPI, MISSOURI, NIGER, NILE, OHIO,

AMAZON, AMUR, COLORADO, COLUMBIA, CONGO, CUMBERLAND,

ORINOCO, PO, RED, RHINE, SEINE, TIBER, VISTULA, VOLGA, YUKON.

GO AHEAD... GET YOUR FEET WET! YOU MAY USE ANY OF THESE "RENOWNED RIVERS" CHOICES.

ACROSS

2. Created the Grand Canyon
4. Large one in Venezuela
6. Runs from Krakow to Warsaw to the Baltic Sea
8. Passes through Vienna, Budapest and Belgrade on its way to the Black Sea
9. Longest one in Brazil
12. Runs from St. Louis to New Orleans
16. Goes from Frankfurt to the Netherlands and into the North Sea
17. River of the Pharoahs in Egypt
18. Runs through Nashville, Tennessee
20. Forms the border between Texas and Oklahoma
21. River of Rome, Italy
22. "Gold Rush" river in Canada

DOWN

1. Runs through Zaire, Africa to the Atlantic Ocean
3. Great river of British Columbia
5. Famous for salmon; meets the Pacific Ocean near Portland, Oregon
6. Famous Russian river; goes from Moscow to the Black Sea
7. Forms a border between China and the USSR near the Pacific Ocean
10. Starts at Pittsburgh, Pennsylvania, and ends at Cairo, Illinois
11. River in Nigeria, Africa; starts with the letter N.
12. Flows past Omaha into the Mississippi near St. Louis, Missouri
13. Flows through Paris, France
14. River in Northern Italy
15. Passes from Mandalay in Burma and flows into the Indian Ocean
19. Goes from Dresden in East Germany to Hamburg

COMPASS CONNECTIONS

Connect the numbers by following the directions below. Use a map when necessary.

Draw a line from:

1 to 2 if the Pacific Ocean borders the west coast of North America.

2 to 3 if Hawaii is north of Alaska.

3 to 4 if Australia is south of Greenland.

4 to 5 if Canada is south of Mexico.

5 to 6 if Quebec is east of British Columbia.

6 to 7 if California is west of Kansas.

7 to 8 if Florida is east of Texas.

8 to 9 if Mississippi is southeast of Ohio.

9 to 10 if Oregon is west of West Virginia.

10 to 11 if New York is northwest of Washington, D.C.

11 to 12 if South America is north of the South Pole.

Think About It   Fill in the following.

The Atlantic Ocean borders the _____ coast of Canada.

Greenland is _____ of the United States.

Tennessee is _____ of Michigan.

Nevada is _____ of Utah.

Write 3 factual direction sentences for cities near your home.

_____

_____

_____

LUCKY 13

You may have to work on this one for a long time. In fact, you'll be lucky if you finish it in less than 13 hours. Just keep it around, think about it and work on completing it as you have time.

You'll need pencil and paper, some reference books, a sharp head and plenty of patience.

1) Multiply 13 x 13 x 113 x 1113.

2) Write 13 words that could be used to describe this lady.

3) Find 13 hidden 13's in this picture.

4) In 13 minutes, make up 13 math problems. The answer to each must be 13. (If you don't succeed the first time, keep setting your watch and starting over until you do ... that is, unless you have not succeeded by the 13th try. If this happens, it's time to ask for help.

5) Write 13 words with 13 letters each (we had to use the dictionary for this one).

6) List the names of 13 animals that all begin with the letter "c."

ATTENTION, PUZZLE-LOVERS!

ON EACH OF THE PUZZLE PIECES BELOW, YOU WILL FIND THE NAME AND AUTHOR OF ONE OF THE WORLD'S GREATEST PUZZLE BOOKS.

CUT OUT THE PUZZLE PIECES. ARRANGE AND PASTE THEM ON A SEPARATE SHEET OF PAPER. SAVE YOUR PUZZLE FOR A LIBRARY REFERENCE!

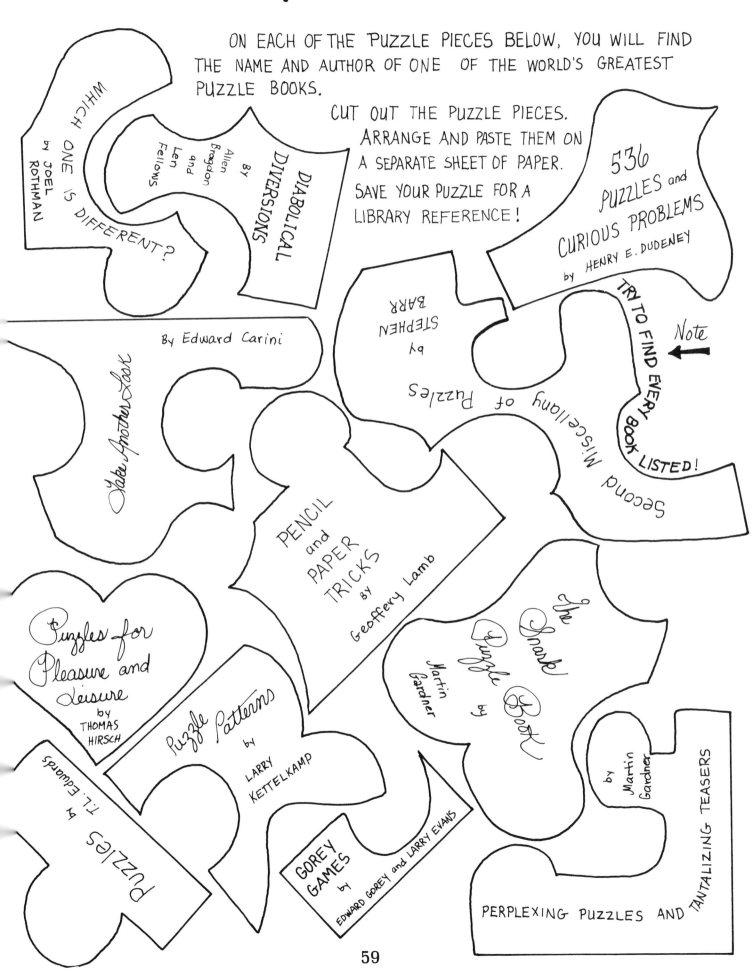

WHICH ONE IS DIFFERENT? by JOEL ROTHMAN

DIABOLICAL DIVERSIONS By Allen Brogdon and Len Fellows

536 PUZZLES and CURIOUS PROBLEMS by HENRY E. DUDENEY

Note — TRY TO FIND EVERY BOOK LISTED!

By Edward Carini

Take Another Look

by STEPHEN BARR

Second Miscellany of Puzzles

PENCIL and PAPER TRICKS by Geoffery Lamb

The Snark Puzzle Book by Martin Gardner

Puzzles for Pleasure and Leisure by THOMAS HIRSCH

Puzzle Patterns by LARRY KETTELKAMP

Puzzles by T.L. Edwards

GOREY GAMES by EDWARD GOREY and LARRY EVANS

by Martin Gardner

PERPLEXING PUZZLES AND TANTALIZING TEASERS

FLYING FREE!

And if your
mind will let
you soar
Like a butterfly
on the wing.

I WISH YOU LUCK

According to an old superstition, a butterfly lighting on your left shoulder brings good luck for the days to come. For this reason, some people walk around in fields of flowers with sugar on the left shoulder to attract butterflies. Other people buy silver or gold butterfly pins and wear them on the left shoulder for luck.

Here's a whole page full of butterflies for you.

Trace and cut out some of these butterflies for special people in your life. Slip up behind each person, pin the butterfly in place and wish him or her good luck.

Don't forget to keep a butterfly for your own left shoulder.

 *(Think About It)*

63

TROLLS in TROUBLE

If you read this story and follow the directions carefully, you will complete a beautiful picture. To make a wall poster for your room, just glue your finished picture onto a sheet of construction paper, and hang it up.

Many years ago, the trolls who inhabited this beautiful forest retreat received some terrible news. A horde of cruel giants was invading the countryside, heading straight for their land. In desperation, they called on Mojo the Magician to help them. So Mojo cast a magic spell that removed all color and shape from the forest to hide it from the giants.

Through his art, Mojo knew that the giants would eventually be driven out of the forest. Using his magic powers, Mojo worked out a number code in the hope that a hero would someday come along to restore the forest retreat. Until that time, the trolls and their forest would remain colorless and shapeless.

Can you help? Use your crayons and this code to bring color and shape back to the trolls' world shown on the next page.

If 6 x 9 = 54, color the #1 spaces purple.

If 5 x 8 = 40, color the #2 spaces brown.

If 7 x 4 = 28, color the #3 spaces red.

If 3 x 12 = 38, color the #4 spaces purple.

If 8 x 7 = 65, color the #5 spaces pink.

If 4 x 6 = 24, color the #6 spaces brown.

If 9 x 8 = 72, color the #7 spaces dark green.

If 12 x 3 = 36, color the #8 spaces light green.

If 11 x 6 = 66, color the #9 spaces pink.

If 8 x 6 = 48, color the #10 spaces sky blue.

If 11 x 10 = 101, color the #12 spaces tan.

If 7 x 5 = 35, color the #12 spaces dark green.

If 6 x 7 = 49, color the #14 spaces red.

If 12 x 5 = 60, color the #14 spaces yellow.

If 5 x 9 = 54, color the #16 spaces brown.

If 3 x 7 = 21, color the #16 spaces light green.

If 4 x 8 = 32, color the #17 spaces sky blue.

If 6 x 6 = 63, color the #20 spaces pink.

If 9 x 9 = 90, color the #20 spaces dark green.

If 12 x 10 = 120, color the #20 spaces tan.

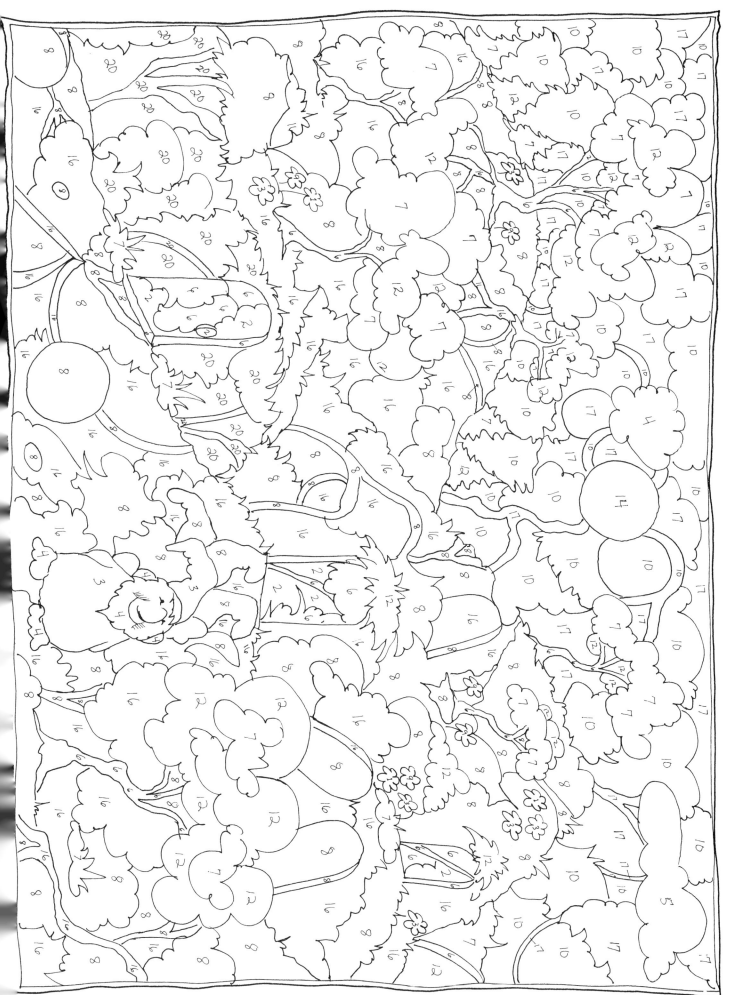

A Friend To Trolls Deserves A Treat!

FOR BEING A GOOD FRIEND TO TROLLS IN NEED, YOU ARE AWARDED THE PRIVILEGE OF SELECTING ONE OF THE FOLLOWING "THINK ABOUT IT" TREATS. CIRCLE THE ACTIVITY TREAT OF YOUR CHOICE, AND COMPLETE IT ON ANOTHER SHEET OF PAPER.

Think About It

1. Write the most exciting tall tale you can think of to tell of the trolls' return to their homeland.

2. Make up a special menu and list of games and contests for the trolls' celebration banquet.

3. Draw finger puppets to represent a troll family returning to the forest. Color them and cut them out. Then, write a conversation they might have, and "let your fingers do the walking."

4. Use the following words to make a jigsaw, a word search or a crossword puzzle for a friend to solve.

trolls	retreat	spell	help
magic	hiding	cast	forest
shape	code	invading	giants
someday	restore	inhabit	hero

What IS This?

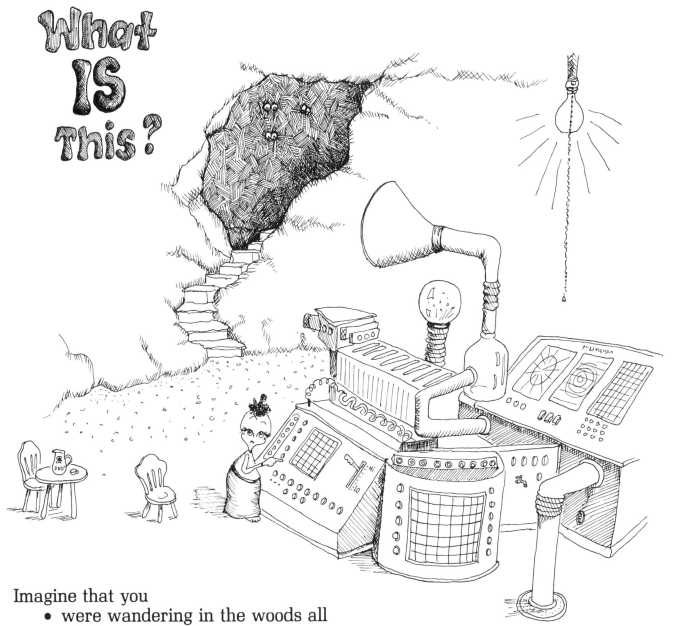

Imagine that you
- were wandering in the woods all alone on a hot summer day ...
- stepped in a hole in the ground ...
- felt yourself sliding on a real slide — down, down, down ...
- suddenly landed on your feet in a huge, brightly lit cave!

And, as your eyes became accustomed to the glare, you saw this scene.

What in the world would you do?

How would you find out where you are and what this strange machine is?

Think About It

On a separate sheet of paper, write 20 good questions that you would ask. Since you may use only 20, you will want to word each question very carefully.

BEHIND CLOSED DOORS

JUST PRETEND...

Your teacher leaves the room.

When the door closes behind her, it becomes totally stuck.

Everyone in the room tries to open it.

The teacher, the principal & the custodian try to open it from the hall, but cannot.

Everyone, both inside and outside, tries to open the windows, but they are all stuck, too.

The fire department and the police are summoned to rescue the students, but to no avail.

Finally, all signs of life outside the room cease.

The electricity in the room is off, its dark, and only you and your class-mates are left in the building. What will happen now?

Think About It

Which three of your classmates would you expect to take over and offer a survival plan for the night?

1)_____ 2)_____ 3)_____

Of these three, whose plan would you expect to be most practical?

_____

Of these three, whose plan would you expect to be most creative?

_____

Which three of your classmates would you expect to provide entertainment to keep the class from panicing?

1)_____ 2)_____ 3)_____

Of these three, whose entertainment would you expect to be most successful?

_____

Of these three, whose entertainment would you expect to be most creative?

_____

On the back of your paper, give good reasons for each of your choices.

What would YOU do?

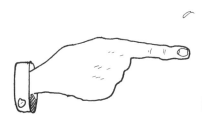

If the door really did close on your classroom, and you and your classmates really were locked inside, and all the people on the outside were unable to help, what would YOU do?

Quickly write three sentences to tell what you would do.

_____

_____

_____

Number the sentences (1, 2 and 3) to show the order in which you would do them.

Reread your sentences as ordered.

Does your plan make good sense to you? _____

Is there something you left out or need to add?_____

If so, add it here.

_____

_____

What person would you ask to help you carry out the plan?

_____ Why? _____

_____

Discuss your plan with someone whose judgment you trust. Ask for his/her suggestions, and for an opinion related to your plan's chance for success.

No Happy Ending In Sight

Read the unfinished story below. Then, write an ending to make it a very bad day indeed for poor George.

Think About It

As George took his brand new ice skates from the box, he was thinking about the wonderful time he would have skating on the ice-covered pond in the park around the corner. He rushed to the phone to call his friend Josef to ask him to meet him at the pond. Josef's mother answered the phone and told George that Josef was in bed with the mumps. She reminded George that he and Josef had been together every day for the past two weeks, including yesterday when Josef was beginning to complain about being hot and having a very sore throat. She said that since George had most certainly been exposed to the mumps, maybe he should stay home today.

George's throat did feel strange, and when he opened the door to put his dog out, the cold air made it feel worse. He was so anxious to try his new skates, however, that he decided to go on to the park. In his haste, he forgot his gloves and he couldn't remember where he had left his hat and muffler the night before.

He ran all the way to the park because he wanted to be on the ice before the other kids arrived. When he got there, he noticed a sign at the pond's edge, but just didn't take time to stop and read it. His head was hurting and he really felt hot and out of breath when he got to the pond, but he hastily strapped on his skates and rushed onto the ice.

_____

_____

_____

_____

_____

_____

_____

Write a Sad Story

Think About It

Read the last paragraph of LuAnne's story, and write the beginning and middle of it. Tell why and how poor LuAnne managed to find herself in such a sad situation.

LuAnne saw her friends disappear around the corner. As she looked down at her bleeding knee, her scattered books and her torn skirt, she thought about the events of the past hour and began to cry. "If only I had obeyed my mother, used my head, and treated my friends a little more kindly, none of this would have happened," she said.

EVERYBODY Has a Bad Day
Once In A While

Think about a really bad day you once had.
Try to remember just exactly what happened and why it was so bad.
Write a brief paragraph telling about the events of that day.

Reread your paragraph, and in one sentence, state the real problem that caused your day to be such an unhappy one.

Could you have done something to avoid the problem or to prevent the same thing from happening again?
Write one sentence to tell what you could have done, or why you could have done nothing to change the situation.

POWERFUL
THINKING

Look up the word "power" in the dictionary and read the definition given. In your own words, write its meaning.

power — _____

_____

_____

_____

Beside each word below, write a sentence that uses that word and tells of its power or of the consequences of that power.

politics — _____

_____

storm — _____

_____

tradition — _____

_____

education — _____

_____

fear — _____

_____

electricity — _____

_____

love — _____

_____

gossip — _____

_____

prejudice — _____

_____

WHAT WOULD'VE HAPPENED

Use three sentences or less to tell what would have happened if

... all the barnyard animals had worked together to help the Little Red Hen bake bread.

_____

_____

_____

_____

_____

... Isabella, the Queen of Spain, had refused to finance Columbus's voyage to the New World.

_____

_____

_____

_____

_____

_____

_____

... the printing press had never been invented. _____

_____

_____

_____

_____

_____

CAPTIONS COUNT

On a separate sheet of paper, write two good cartoon captions for this picture.

What are the implications of each caption you have written? Decide which is more creative, and use that caption as the starter for a brief creative story.

Compare the thoughts conveyed by the caption and the story. Which is more interesting? Why?

A LAUGH A DAY!

Did you know that a laugh a day can help people stay healthy, and that sometimes, laughter helps sick people get well?

Think About It

For starters, finish the "Laughs" on this page. Then, finish the "Laugh-A-Day" calendar on the following page. Write a corny joke, a riddle, a knock-knock, a cartoon, a tongue twister, or whatever it takes to tickle your funny bone in each of the seven spaces. Add fun illustrations, and give your finished calendar to someone who needs a good laugh.

(Note: mailing it with a "your secret pal who wishes you a good laugh" signature will make it even more fun for your special person.)

Why did the motorcycle gang cross the interstate?

_____
_____
_____
_____
_____
_____

What did the Papa Screech-Owl say to the baby Screech-Owl on the way to the skating rink?

_____
_____
_____
_____

KNOCK, KNOCK.
  Who's there?
OTTER.
  Otter who?
YOU OTTER _____

_____
_____
_____

Looks like:

_____
_____
_____

LAUGH-A-DAY CALENDAR

HA!
SUNDAY

HO!
MONDAY

HEE!
TUESDAY

YUK!
WEDNESDAY

HA-HA
THURSDAY

CHUCKLE
FRIDAY

GRIN!
SATURDAY

Where Do You Think Butterflies Go When It Rains?

SHOW YOUR IDEAS HERE.

POSITIVE & NEGATIVE Currents

Read the words below. Imagine how each would look if you used just one crayon and one line to illustrate it. (Give yourself extra flexibility by varying the shape and thickness of each line.)

Celebration   Growth   Despair

Selfishness   Joy   Frustration

Appreciation   Fear   Disgrace

Anticipation   Responsibility   Infinity   Corruption   Immaturity

Beauty   Yesterday   Gratitude   Indecision   Youth   Success

Choose three words that you think express positive feelings, and three words that express negative ones. In the box below, make a collage using the lines you have imagined for those words.

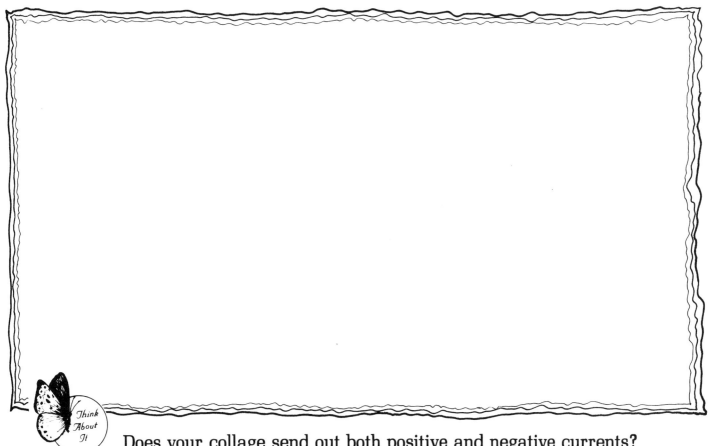

Think About It

Does your collage send out both positive and negative currents?

A Checklist For Butterfly Lovers and Other Creative Kids

Check these off as you remember to ...

_____ Take long walks with time just for thinking. In the woods or beside a stream is best, but it's amazing how much thinking you can do while walking on a busy sidewalk or down a crowded path in a city park.

_____ Collect good junk for collages, gifts, projects and just to enjoy owning.

_____ Keep pencils and paper handy always. The most creative thoughts come to you in the strangest places and at the most undreamed-of times.

_____ Listen to good music often.

_____ Be a list maker. Write down things to do, helps for school, brain teasers, dreams — and lists of lists to make.

_____ Use the dictionary, thesaurus, encyclopedia, atlas, almanac and other reference books.

_____ Select your television programs carefully.

_____ Find some smart people whose conversation you enjoy, and manage to talk with them often.

_____ Develop and enjoy one special hobby. Change your hobby whenever you wish, but stick with one long enough to know if it's for you.

_____ Pick out one sport to participate in. Hang in there, at least until you're sure you've given it your best try.

Write:

_____ Letters (to friends, relatives, pen pals, your teacher or for free stuff)

_____ Stories (mysteries, tall tales, silly or serious ones, fables)

_____ Poems of all kinds

_____ Songs (even if nobody sings them except you)

_____ Jokes, puns, tongue twisters

_____ A personal diary (to learn more than even you want to know about yourself)

_____ Reports (ones you want to do as well as those you have to do)

_____ Maybe even a novel (if you're brave and persevering!)

_____ Start a collection, but don't hesitate to chuck it and start over. Your interests will change if you

Think About It

_____ Use your library card often.

_____ Experiment with all kinds of art materials — tempera and finger paints, crayons, charcoal, chalk; butcher, construction, tissue and drawing paper; and anything else you can get.

_____ Try crafts. Cook, build with wood and nails, sew, knit, macrame, paint, sculpt — all these encourage you to flex your brain.

_____ Find a special spot for daydreaming — a swing, a quiet corner, a tree top or wherever you wish. Just make sure it's convenient enough for you to use it a lot.

81

PICTURE POWER!

This is how one artist pictures these two well-known idioms.

"He's just blowing off steam."

"I'm still waiting for my ship to come in."

 *Think About It* Select one of the following idioms, and make a clever drawing to show how you picture it.

— What he says to me goes in one ear and out the other.
— I refuse to be called on the carpet.
— I'm in a pretty pickle.

Write 4 idioms you would be able to picture in a clever way.

1. _____
_____

2. _____
_____

3. _____
_____

4. _____
_____

BOOKS TO HELP SMART KIDS GET SMARTER
AND CREATIVE KIDS BECOME
MORE CREATIVE

Great for a hot, dull day ...
     Perfect for a cold and dreary day ...
          Especially good when you're sick in bed.
Try one on a rainy day ...
     Choose one for a snowbound stay ...
          Or just any old time you're bored.

Answer Key

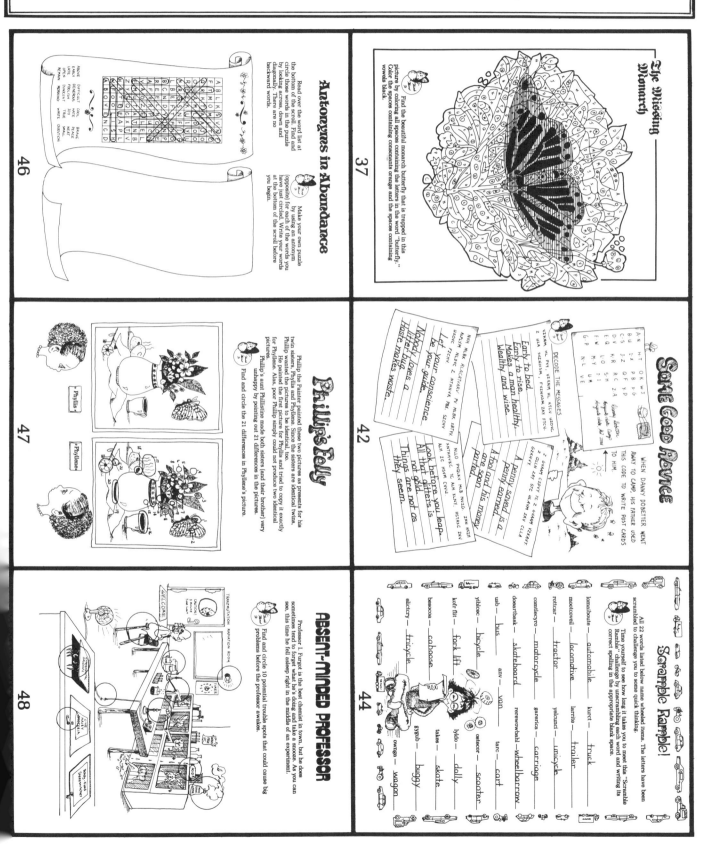

Answer Key

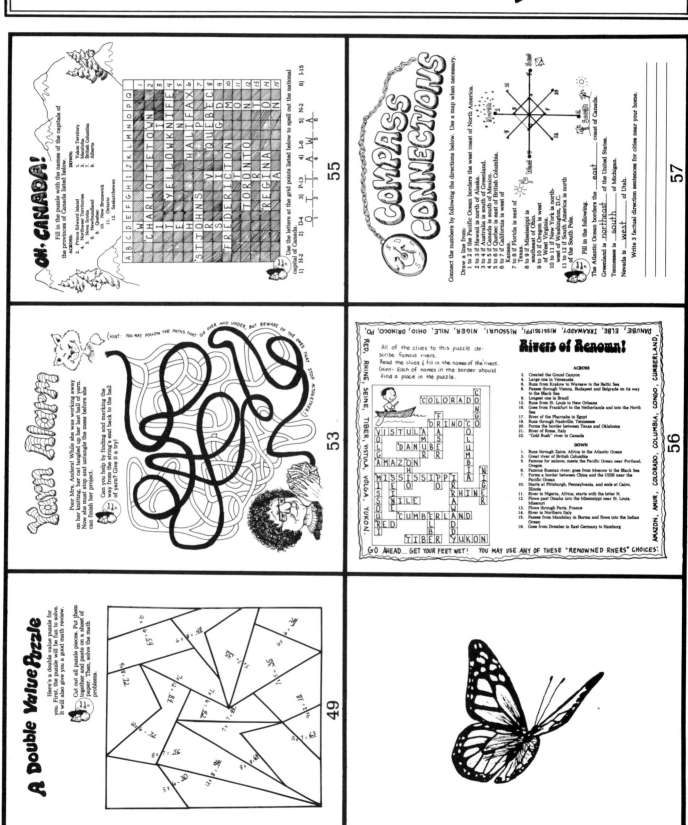

OH, CANADA!

Fill in the puzzle with the names of the capitals of the provinces of Canada listed below.

ACROSS:
2. Prince Edward Island
4. Northwest Territories
6. Nova Scotia
8. Newfoundland
10. Quebec
11. Ontario
12. Saskatchewan

DOWN:
1. Yukon Territory
3. Manitoba
7. British Columbia
9. Alberta

Use the letters at the grid points listed below to spell out the national capital of Canada.

1) H-2 2) D4 3) P-13 4) T-9 5) N-2 6) I-15

O T T A W A

55

COMPASS CONNECTIONS

Connect the numbers by following the directions below. Use a map when necessary.

Draw a line from:
1 to 2 if the Pacific Ocean borders the west coast of North America.
2 to 3 if Hawaii is north of Alaska.
3 to 4 if Australia is south of Greenland.
4 to 5 if Canada is south of Mexico.
5 to 6 if Quebec is east of British Columbia.
6 to 7 if California is west of Kansas.
7 to 8 if Florida is east of Texas.
8 to 9 if Mississippi is southeast of Ohio.
9 to 10 if Oregon is west of West Virginia.
10 to 11 if New York is north-west of Washington, D.C.
11 to 12 if South America is north of the South Pole.

Fill in the following.
The Atlantic Ocean borders the **east** coast of Canada.
Greenland is **northeast** of the United States.
Tennessee is **south** of Michigan.
Nevada is **west** of Utah.

Write 3 factual direction sentences for cities near your home.

57

Yarn Alarm

Poor Mrs. Anders! While she was working away on her knitting, her cat tangled up her last ball of yarn. Now she must stop and untangle the mess before she can finish her project.

Can you help by finding and marking the way from the string's end back to the ball of yarn? Give it a try!

(HINT: YOU MAY FOLLOW THE PATHS THAT GO OVER AND UNDER, BUT BEWARE OF THE ONES THAT STOP AUTO ENTER!)

53

Rivers of Renown!

All of the clues to this puzzle describe famous rivers.

Read the clues & fill in the names of the rivers. (Hint- Each of names in the border should find a place in the puzzle.

ACROSS
2. Created the Grand Canyon
4. Large one in Venezuela
6. Runs from Krakow to Warsaw to the Baltic Sea
8. Passes through Vienna, Budapest and Belgrade on its way to the Black Sea
9. Longest one in Brazil
12. Runs from St. Louis to New Orleans
16. Goes from Frankfurt to the Netherlands and into the North Sea
17. River of the Pharoahs in Egypt
18. Runs through Nashville, Tennessee
20. Forms the border between Texas and Oklahoma
21. River of Rome, Italy
22. "Gold Rush" river in Canada

DOWN
1. Runs through Zaire, Africa to the Atlantic Ocean
3. Great river of British Columbia
5. Famous for salmon; meets the Pacific Ocean near Portland, Oregon
6. Famous Russian river; goes from Moscow to the Black Sea
7. Forms a border between China and the USSR near the Pacific Ocean
10. Starts at Pittsburgh, Pennsylvania, and ends at Cairo, Illinois
11. River in Nigeria, Africa; starts with the letter N.
12. Flows past Omaha into the Mississippi near St. Louis, Missouri
13. Flows through Paris, France
14. River in Northern Italy
15. Passes from Mandalay in Burma and flows into the Indian Ocean
19. Goes from Dresden in East Germany to Hamburg

DANUBE, ELBE, IRRAWADDY, MISSISSIPPI, MISSOURI, NIGER, NILE, OHIO, ORINOCO, PO, RED, RHINE, SEINE, TIBER, VISTULA, VOLGA, YUKON.

AMAZON, AMUR, COLORADO, COLUMBIA, CONGO, CUMBERLAND,

GO AHEAD... GET YOUR FEET WET!   YOU MAY USE ANY OF THESE "RENOWNED RIVERS" CHOICES!

56

A Double Value Puzzle

Here's a double value puzzle for you. First, the puzzle will be fun to solve. It will also give you a good math review.

Cut out all puzzle pieces. Put them together and paste on a sheet of paper. Then, solve the math problems.

49